# {NAVIGATING WELLNESS}

## Creating an effective strategy for cost containment

By:

Johnette van Eeden, CEO of Star Wellness®

*Live life well !! :)*
*Johnette*

# «. Praise for Navigating Wellness .»

"This is a well-written book that presents both facts and conclusions for companies considering ways to improve their workers' health. While the author is in the business of medical screening, she expands the horizon by detailing ways of fostering health beyond screening. Good health is not merely a numbers game, but numbers do guide employees to necessary next steps and modified lifestyles." – Kym B, Risk Manager

"Johnette hit it out of the ballpark—this book is brilliant. It makes a great case for implementing a corporate wellness program. I presented copies to our directors and they agreed to institute a program and get started right away. This book proved the perfect stimulus to get the executives to act." – Sean T, Business Owner

"Kudos to the author who carefully and consistently provides the information needed to encourage c-suite acceptance and implementation of onsite employee wellness screenings. It is a good read and an invaluable guide. – Mark J, HR Director

# «. Foreword .»

"It's always refreshing to know someone who truly enjoys helping others, a strategic thinker who likes to problem solve. Johnette is a rare find in this area. She always perseveres, with an unstoppable determination to succeed and help others to succeed as well.

This book is well-written and builds an irrefutable case on why companies need to provide wellness screening services onsite for employees. Armed with the knowledge of the issues facing their group of employees allows forward-thinking companies to develop a strategic, customized program designed to address those specific needs.

Follow the program and the results can help create a healthier and more productive workforce and help improve the company's bottom line. It's a win-win!

I do it for myself, my family, and my employees...you should too. Read this book and get started. Your employees and your stockholders will thank you."

Tony Jeary - The RESULTS Guy™

www.tonyjeary.com.

# «. Preface .»

## A definitive, trend-setting guide to corporate wellness

The U.S. workforce continues to be unhealthy and insurance premiums continue to rise year after year.

This statement has been received loud and clear and now corporations, especially large ones, are stepping up to the plate and providing wellness initiatives to benefit their employees.

The reality is that a well-designed wellness program can go a long way in creating a healthier and more productive workforce, while reducing claim costs. Once claims are reduced, premiums reduce as well.

The scale of most programs is expanding exponentially as human resource managers and C-suite executives recognize that people are their most precious commodity and asset.

With this expansion from a first aid kit and worker safety practices to onsite fitness centers, immunizations, and screening for major diseases, corporations are setting the bar high. As a result, employees are healthier, happier, more productive, and tend to stay in their jobs longer.

It's a win-win for everyone. And it's a direct positive return on investment for the corporate bottom line.


Johnette van Eeden, CEO of Star Wellness®

Imagine a company
Where employee health is a primary focus
The recognition that people come first
A place where well-being
Stands at the forefront
Of everything…so the business
Runs better, faster, and stronger…
Yours

# «. Introduction .»

This timely book is about the trend toward comprehensive workplace wellness programs. When properly structured and implemented, these initiatives have a huge positive impact on employee health and a major reduction in the cost of medical claims.

Human resource directors and benefits managers are taking note, as this new reality is vital for the health of employees as well as the financial health of the companies for which they work. Corporate wellness programs consistently result in healthier employee populations. And more often than not, these programs more than pay for themselves.

The relevance of this book is inescapable. With health costs soaring, the more an incidence of disease can be avoided or minimized, the more productive the workforce, the happier the employees, and the greater a company's cost savings. All this leads to an impressive return on investment (ROI) for corporate wellness.

Biometric numbers for employees are measurable, as are the cost savings for companies that implement wellness programs. While the numbers play an important part, benefits go way beyond monetary savings to increased goodwill and workplace satisfaction.

This book reveals the importance of corporate wellness

in worksites, and also provides information for employees about their part in the process—through awareness, knowledge, education, and incremental lifestyle modifications, employees hold the keys to their own and their companies' well-being.

The message must reach upper management too, as executive engagement is essential for the success of corporate wellness programs. Without support from those at the top, most employees will not feel like the program is important. But if the CEO is out walking with employees and counting steps, or personally handing out rewards and incentives to those who reach goals and milestones, employees become more engaged.

This book is indispensable for those in leadership positions, managers, and others looking to improve the experience of the places we spend the majority of our waking hours—our jobs, our careers, our workplace communities.

# Table of Contents

# Chapter 1 - Basic Facts

## 1.1 What exactly is wellness?

There is wellness and there is corporate wellness. For the first, it is loosely defined as an individual being healthy. For the second, it originally began as employee safety and efforts to prevent injuries in the workplace.

This definition has expanded to include the physical, emotional, financial, and psychological well-being of employees both in the workplace and in their private lives. After all, lifestyle impacts employee productivity, and physical and emotional health play large parts in the ability of an employee to do his or her work effectively and consistently.

Rising healthcare costs, government regulations surrounding corporate insurance coverage for the workforce, and competitive hiring and retention realities have made corporate wellness a necessity rather than a luxury.

But how best to strategize and implement this new normal?

## 1.2 The Rationale behind corporate wellness programs

According to the CDC, rising health care costs are unsustainable. Companies must take action to head off rising healthcare costs. Workplace wellness, including onsite screenings, is proven to help with cost avoidance.

For the past three decades, the Department of Health and Human Services (HHS) has issued a national agenda aimed at improving the health of all Americans over each 10-year span. Under each of these Healthy People initiatives, HHS established health targets and monitored how well people were reaching them over time. Healthy People 2020 lays out the proposed agenda for the current decade, which will end in 2020.

Outline strategies with objectives to support them grouped into 3 categories:

1.  preventive services
2.  intervention
3.  healthy lifestyle promotion

The U.S. Preventive Services Task Force (USPSTF), recommends a set of clinical preventive services that are determined in part by age, sex, and presence of specific known risk factors. Maciosek and colleagues (2010) found that an increase in the use of clinical preventive services could result in more than 2 million life-years saved annually in the United States.

Furthermore, they found that "increasing the use of these services from current levels to 90 percent in 2006 would result in total savings of $3.7 billion." The National Commission on Prevention Priorities (2007) found that utilization rates of recommended, cost-effective preventive services remains low and that "increasing the use of just five preventive services would save more than 100,000 lives each year in the United States."

Although once optional, corporate wellness programs have fast become the standard. Under The Affordable Care Act (ACA), preventive screenings are covered at 100% by insurance plans, not subject to deductibles. By exempting preventive services from having any out of pocket costs, more individuals receive preventive care.

Healthcare costs are on a continual rise and the ability to hire and retain qualified personnel is increasingly competitive. A recent Society for Human Resource Management (SHRM) study shows year by year growth in the number of companies incorporating wellness programs as a business strategy.

The 2010 Harvard study *Workplace Wellness Programs Can Generate Savings*, shows medical costs fall $3.27 for every dollar spent on wellness programs, and absentee day costs fall by $2.73 for every dollar spent. According to the abstract of this study, "this return on investment suggests that the wider adoption of such programs could prove beneficial for budgets and productivity as well as health outcomes."

With time constraints ever-present, providing employees with onsite preventive services saves time for individuals and boosts workplace productivity. A well-designed program is not only a superb way of ensuring a healthier and more productive workforce, but can also save lives through early detection and prevention of disease.

It has been shown time and time again that human nature is affected by others who surround you. It follows that competition and healthy life choices are contagious. If the person in the cubicle or office next to you is out walking at lunchtime, or eating a salad rather than a burger and fries, you are more likely to make good choices too.

If everyone in your department is getting a flu shot during the onsite clinic and it only takes five minutes and does not cost you anything, you are much more likely to schedule your five minutes and get a shot too. Absenteeism decreases as there is no time lost from work traveling somewhere to get the shot. And once they have had their shots, employees are less likely to take time off because their chances of contracting the flu are minimized.

If screening for high blood pressure, heart disease, and

diabetes (among other chronic diseases) can be done in a 5 to 10 minute appointment in the workplace with a positive return on investment (ROI), implementing such screening and testing is a no brainer.

Psychological needs, competition, fear reduction, convenience and low or no cost, all play roles. Strategically targeting employee needs, desires, and emotional triggers makes implementation and maintenance of a wellness program more successful over a longer time.

Smoking and alcohol cessation programs are effective too. Everyone knows that smoking is bad for your health, yet it is the most preventable cause of heart disease. Employees that smoke have two to four times more chance of heart disease, and the longer a person smokes, the greater the risk. According to the CDC, almost 20% of deaths from heart disease are caused by smoking. Alcohol not only causes premature aging, but also damages the liver and other organs of the body. These programs have come a long way, as have wellness programs in general, and the health benefits are huge.

## 1.3 Lifestyle changes triggered by outside influences

Human nature is such that adults, especially coworkers,

are often competitive. This competition is within the individuals themselves — when someone wants to better themselves, their records, or their health statistics. This same competition is also with others, especially those around them, such as family members, friends, and coworkers.

Pedometers and the newer incarnation of Fit bits and Apple watches, Smartphone apps, and other tech gadgets enable us to track our activity and progress, and to compete with ourselves and with others.

Setting up contests and awards, as well as incentives, will often jumpstart a new corporate wellness program or otherwise inject excitement into an existing program. Adding a dose of healthy competition to a weight loss program often increases results, even more so when part of a team.

Behavioral change is never easy. Initial good intentions level off. However, positive feedback, especially when health is concerned, pays off in goodwill, a happier workforce, increased productivity, and cost savings.

## 1.4 Improvements in business productivity

Healthy workers are happier and happiness impacts productivity. It also keeps employees working longer and harder for companies that show they care by providing and encouraging wellness. Research from Towers Watson and the National Business Group showed how "organizations with highly effective wellness programs report significantly lower voluntary attrition than do those whose programs have low effectiveness (9% vs. 15%)."

And healthy workers help lower a firm's healthcare costs, insurance premiums, absenteeism, and employee fear of disease—all in all, an excellent return on investment (ROI).

Check these statistics for the leading causes of death in the United States:

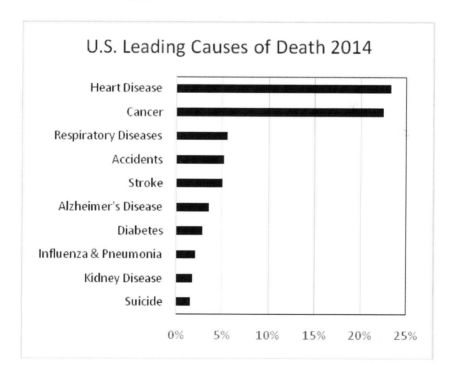

## 1.5 Workplace wellness initiatives

These organized programs are sponsored by employers to benefit and support employee behavior. The goals are to reduce health risks, encourage and incentivize behaviors that improve quality of life, and thereby increase employee productivity, reduce absenteeism, and dramatically decrease healthcare costs, thus improving the organization's bottom line.

# Chapter 2 - Why Test at Work?

## 2.1 Screening and assessments — how they benefit corporate wellness

Screening and assessments constitute a major component of a successful workplace wellness program. Outsourcing these services is easy and cost effective.

Onsite testing is safe, minimally invasive, and an easy to implement aspect of a wellness program.

The screening provides information on potential medical issues that can lead to early detection and/or disease prevention. In both scenarios, employees benefit and so does the company.

Quality control, privacy, and quick reporting of results are important facets of doing this properly.

The types of testing generally include screening for cholesterol, glucose, blood pressure, waist circumference, and body mass index (BMI). Qualified medical personnel and phlebotomists conduct the screenings. Additional testing can easily be included, depending on budget, to meet the organizational wellness goals.

Encouraging employees to take their results with them to their next doctor appointment also reinforces the program and further reduces cost. The doctor can review the test results and make recommendations in one appointment, saving time for both the doctor and the employee.

Trained personnel can help interpret results and make recommendations for moving forward. These counselors explain the numbers and their ramifications, and deal with a range of employee emotions from fear to relief and from confusion to happiness relevant to test results. A level of trust in the providers, coupled with smooth and professional processes, helps make the screening process user-friendly.

While individual results are confidential, group aggregate reports can help identify problem areas within an organization. Focused wellness initiatives can be designed to address and monitor these areas. Year by year analysis of results and claims also aids in calculating the return on investment (ROI).

## 2.2 What is biometric screening?

Biometric screening is the measurement and analysis of physical attributes as they relate to health and involves statistical calculations of health data, and measurable characteristics to provide details on current and potential medical issues. Screening in the context of corporate wellness involves simple medical tests and measurements designed to reveal employees' health situations and to offer insights into intervention and lifestyle modifications that can improve and prevent the onset of disease. This testing can be done onsite with friendly vendors providing non-invasive tests — merely drawing blood, weighing and measuring individuals, taking blood pressure, and inquiring about alcohol and tobacco usage…a visit only takes a short period of time.

With immediate or timely results (within a few days for blood laboratory analysis), and with compassionate medical personnel on hand, or information available to translate and explain those results, employees are educated about their personal health profile. With options for ameliorating/improving potentially negative numbers, fears and concerns are reduced.

With screening costs covered by employers and testing conducted on-site to reduce time spent getting to and waiting for testing to mere minutes, the process is easy and the logistics are convenient. What's not to like? The better the experience for the employee, the more engaged, more motivated, and more likely they are to participate in the ongoing corporate wellness program…once the employee knows their individual screening results.

## 2.3 Employers are taking note

In companies with more than 200 employees, 90 percent of these large firms have already instituted wellness programs of various kinds. The trend is for the rest, as well as medium and smaller companies, to start programs too. A recent SHRM study showed that 80% of companies without a wellness program were interested in starting one within the next 3 years.

There is also a need for the large employers with existing programs to expand and improve those programs to keep employees engaged and motivated. Initial excitement is one thing; maintenance and adhering are quite another.

Certain trends are emerging. Participation levels are no longer the only measure of success. Results are starting to rule as companies focus on improving metrics to measure the impact of their wellness programs, and structuring incentives accordingly.

There is certainly a focus on obesity, since weight and weight-related problems continue to constitute a growing problem in the U.S. Obesity is classified as having a Body Mass Index, or BMI, of 30 or more. The CDC reports that more than one-third(36.5%) of

American adults and 17% of teens and children are obese, at an annual cost of nearly $200 billion. Obese employee medical care costs are 42% more per year than an employee with a healthy weight.

There is an ongoing focus on smoking too, since smokers cost companies nearly $6,000 a year in healthcare costs. Employers are taking the lead by instituting programs to help individuals stop or change deadly habits. Some companies are even going as far as requiring an all non-smoking workforce. Regulations regarding smoke-free workplace laws vary by state so consult your employment law attorney prior to making changes to avoid a wrongful termination lawsuit.

Leveraging technology for wellness is another ongoing trend. Fitness trackers and workout apps can help employees track everything from calories to cardio. We all love to keep score, so using technology to help us do so easily becomes part of a corporate wellness program. Our love of gadgets can make exercise and nutrition much less onerous; it can even make it fun.

Corporate cafeterias are now carrying healthier menu options and smaller portions. Some companies are even subsidizing the healthier options and charging more for unhealthier ones. One study showed when fruit and vegetable costs were lowered 50%, purchases increased 300%. Employers are also providing healthier snacks at meetings and company-sponsored social events. Stop the donuts and pizza!

The bottom line is that employers understand a healthy workforce is good for business, so they are increasingly taking a leadership role in the entire realm of employee wellness.

You only have to look at the data for adults in the United States to see why. According to a Department of Health and Human Services 2007 report for every 100 employees:

- 44 Suffer from Stress
- 38 Overweight
- 31 Use Alcohol Excessively
- 30 High Cholesterol
- 26 High Blood Pressure
- 25 Heart Disease
- 24 Do not Exercise
- 21 Smoke
- 20 Do not wear seat belts
- 12 Asthmatic
- 6 Diabetic

# Chapter 3 Rewards & Incentives

## 3.1 Implementing incentives and disincentives

Lose weight? Great, that is an incentive. Lower your blood pressure? What a wonderful idea. For some, a health goal is sufficient to motivate behavior change. But for others, enthusiasm may not be there, or it may be insufficient to maintain interest. Take all the employees who start off in a program, and there will be a large percentage who drop out prior to completion.

Rewards, even simple ones, all help. Approximately two-thirds of companies offer incentives as part of their wellness strategy. Some examples are water bottles and stress balls, a T-shirt with the company or department name, discounts on gym memberships (unless you have a company fitness center onsite), spa services, gift card for a massage, new pair of athletic shoes, etc. Fit bits or other wearable fitness trackers are the new go-to devices of the moment. Providing them to employees will do a lot for company morale. These gadgets are comfortable enough to wear 24/7. They can track employee activity while awake. And movement sensors monitor quality of sleep to determine whether it is fitful or restful, deep or light.

One of the most popular incentives in recent years is a premium reduction for employees who have an annual screening, be it through their personal doctor or the company sponsored wellness program. While the amount of the reduction may vary by group (from $20 a month to $100 a month or more), a well thought-out program can fund itself.

Disincentives like higher costs for unhealthy foods in the cafeteria or higher premiums for smokers are sometimes effective too.

Outcome-based programs, where rewards are tied to an individual's screening results, are also becoming popular. There are certain requirements surrounding the legality of such programs, including a "reasonable alternative" option for qualification.

The ability of employees to include covered spouses and significant others in the wellness program helps give added support and interest for the initiative.

You will obtain increased buy-in by having a wellness program committee made up of both employees and managers. These committee members become walking and talking advocates of the entire program, which helps boost morale and participation.

Promoting lifestyle changes that result in healthier employees takes more than just incentives. There is no one-size-fits-all incentive solution. Each employer needs to figure out what works best for their culture and population.

## 3.2 Make the program an ongoing priority

Short-term activities need to be followed up by new activities. Having a monthly wellness topic or quarterly offering helps to keep wellness at the forefront of everyone's mind. Small or recurring successes are more helpful than one-off ones. Examples would be cholesterol screenings in February (National Heart Month), a team weight loss contest in the spring, flu shots in the fall, and stroke screenings at year end.

## 3.3 Employee recognition

Acknowledging milestones through certificates or announcements is a motivational tool. A congratulatory message from a manager and/or colleagues is also a positive reinforcement for participation. One of the best examples of this is Lincoln Industries, whose successful program was highlighted on CNN. They have so successfully imbedded wellness into their culture that it is even a part of their annual performance review. Each year, the company sponsors a 14,000 foot mountain climb.

Employees who qualify at the platinum level of their point based program and meet fitness qualifications are invited to join the climb and the team scales the summit together. The company president joins the group as his schedule allows showing his support.

## 3.4 Fostering maximum participation

Find ways to jumpstart a new program or encourage employees who have not participated or have dropped out to get involved again. Rewards and incentives provide a short-term way of inciting interest. Long-term, you need participants to buy in to benefits.

While most companies stop short of making participation mandatory, incentives are often structured in a way that makes participation very attractive. You know your group better than anyone else. Use that knowledge to structure your incentive program and maximize results.

# Chapter 4–The Sinister 7

## 4.1 Overview

Most people do not realize that only 5% of the population in any group accounts for 50% of total healthcare expenses, and that there are really only about 15 healthcare conditions that account for over 44% of the total healthcare cost.

Providing on-site medical screening can help address this problem with early detection and prevention of disease. When structured correctly, you can screen onsite for seven of the top ten healthcare expense categories in a simple 8-10 minute appointment. We call these the sinister 7.

Intentionally designing your corporate wellness programs this way is smart and helps with cost containment. Increasing medical costs are debilitating companies nationwide; each year more companies drop benefits completely because the annual premium increase is in the double digit range.

As we all know, there have been significant changes in healthcare law the past few years. There is a lot of cost shifting going on, and many employees can no longer afford to participate in the company health plan because their portion of the premium is too high. Deductibles are also outrageous. It is called the Affordable Care Act but for many people there is nothing affordable about it.

How do you know what screenings to offer to employees? That is what we hope to help you understand in this chapter. We are going to talk about the top expenditures in healthcare and what onsite screenings can help with early detection and prevention.

## 4.2 Heart Disease

Do you know the very first symptom of one-third of all heart attacks that occur each day? Most people say chest pain or numbness in the arms. No, it is not that at all. The alarming answer is that the very first symptom is instant death!

Cardiovascular disease is caused by plaque, or blockage, in the arteries. If the artery leads to the heart, it is a heart attack. If the artery leads to the brain, it is called a stroke.

Cardiovascular disease is the number one killer of both men and women in the world. According to the

Department of Health and Human Services, for every 100 employees, you can bet that at least 25 of them have heart disease.

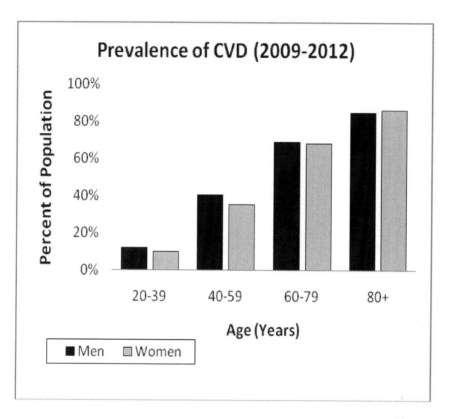

Heart disease is the leading cause of death for both men and women. For women, breast cancer gets all the press, but women actually have a far higher chance of dying from heart disease than breast cancer.

Studies show that if a woman goes to the emergency room with chest pain, she routinely receives different care than a man presenting with the same concern. With a man, a heart attack is automatically assumed, whereas for a woman, other conditions, such as indigestion or hormones, are often looked at first. Even though more men will have heart attacks, more women will die from them because of the difference in care.

Heart disease, stroke and other cardiovascular disease are responsible for one in three deaths. That means that one American is dying every 40 seconds from cardiovascular disease, and one every 90 seconds from heart disease alone.

According to the *2015 Heart Disease and Stroke Statistics Update* for 2015, an American suffers a heart attack about every 43 seconds. The latest statistics for cardiovascular disease direct and indirect cost in the U.S. is more than $320 billion. This translates to 70% of all healthcare costs.

The most popular screening for heart disease is cholesterol. Screening is done from a blood sample, either by drawing a blood sample with a needle, or a finger stick. Cholesterol is not the cause of heart disease but it is considered to be a symptom, especially in the U.S. where cholesterol-lowering medications, or statins, are widely prescribed.

Another onsite screening for cardiovascular disease is C-reactive protein, or CRP. New data shows that increased CRP levels correlate to increased heart disease risk. This is important data because half of all heart attacks happen in people with normal cholesterol levels.

Results from the Harvard Women's Health study show that CRP testing is more accurate than cholesterol in predicting heart disease. Screening for CRP is also done from a blood sample, and can be collected at the same time as other blood tests.

Homocysteine is another blood marker that has been linked to heart disease. Homocysteine is an amino acid normally found in the blood that is produced as your body digests and breaks down protein. High homocysteine concentrations can damage the lining of blood vessels, making them susceptible to plaque build-up and eventual blockage.

Homocysteine appears to be associated with thickening, narrowing and scarring along the inside of the walls of the arteries, as well as higher LDL ("bad") cholesterol levels and the formation of blood clots.

Homocysteine can be effectively lowered by taking B vitamins and eating folic acid fortified foods. This screening is also useful in patients with a family history but no other known risk factors.

## 4.3 – Stroke

Stroke is number two on our list of the sinister 7. The National Stroke Association calls stroke a "brain attack" because it occurs when there is a blockage or rupture in an artery leading to the brain, resulting in the brain not getting the blood it needs to survive. A lot of people confuse stroke and heart attacks.

Stroke is the fifth leading cause of death in America and the leading cause of adult disability. One stroke occurs approximately every 40 seconds, taking a life every four minutes in the U.S.

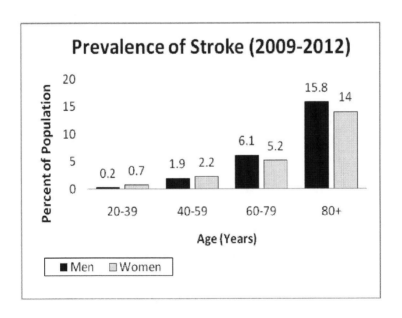

There are two different types of strokes; hemorrhagic and ischemic. A hemorrhagic stroke occurs when a blood vessel in the brain bursts, resulting in blood spilling into the brain. High blood pressure and aneurysms can cause this type of stroke.

An ischemic stroke is the most common type of stroke and happens when an artery to the brain becomes blocked, or occluded, by plaque or a blood clot.

Women are twice as likely to die from stroke as breast cancer. 80% of all strokes are actually preventable through early detection screening. There are approximately 800,000 strokes each year in the U.S. alone.

The cost for stroke in the U.S. from 2010 was $73.7 billion. If you survive a stroke, there is often a lot of expense surrounding ongoing care due to possible brain damage.

It is very important to get to the ER quickly if you think you are having a stroke as there is a very limited time window to be treated with clot busting drugs that help restore blood flow to the brain.

The carotid artery comes up from the heart and splits, or bifurcates, in the neck into the internal and external carotid arteries. You have both on each side of your neck. The external carotid arteries feed your brain and scalp. They can be completely blocked without great concern by your physician.

The internal carotid arteries are of more concern, as they supply blood flow to the brain. If an internal carotid artery becomes 70% or more occluded, a procedure called an endarterectomy, a surgery to remove the plaque deposit and restore normal blood flow to the brain, may be performed.

Obviously, if you can find any possible blockage prior to actually having a stroke and any resulting brain damage, it is better. An onsite screening that can be offered to screen for stroke is an ultrasound of the carotid artery. This painless procedure allows for viewing and visualization of carotid block ages that are responsible for 80% of strokes.

Our company has caught complete blockages with this simple ultrasound and we have several testimonials from people who say the screening saved their lives. In fact, not only did they tell us that, they say their cardiologists told them that as well!

### 4.3.1 – Case studies - Carotid Artery Ultrasound

An ultrasound screening of the carotid arteries is a painless, non-invasive way to screen for stroke. Using state-of-the-art ultrasound technology, the carotid arteries in your neck are viewed to check for plaque formation. Carotid blockage accounts for 80% of all strokes, 50-75% of which could be prevented with screening and education. This is an easy test to offer employees over 35 years of age and is only needed every couple of years.

*"During our vascular ultrasound screenings, the technician noticed a major carotid blockage on one of our employees. After a brief review of the screening and consulting the Radiologist, our employee immediately went to their treating physician's office.*

*Further testing showed a 90% blockage in the carotid artery. This employee was immediately scheduled for surgery and has already implemented lifestyle changes. She is determined to live a healthier life after this narrow miss of something tragic like a stroke.*

*As the Director of Employee Wellness for our organization, I want to personally thank the Star Wellness Employees who chose to go above and beyond, for allowing this person to participate even though she didn't have a scheduled appointment. These fine people also did an EXCELLENT job in talking with the patient to explain the results of the screening in a way that kept things calm and compassionate.*

*Star Wellness truly saved a life that day. Thank you for the outstanding work that you do!" – Chad H.*

## 4.4– Cancer

Cancer is a word that instantly strikes fear into anyone who hears it, but it is not necessarily a death sentence any more. With early detection, there are many treatments that can be very effective.

The CDC reports that in 2010the U.S. spending for cancer was $125 billion. It is the second leading cause of death in the U.S. and there are more than one million new cancers detected each year. Many deaths could be prevented if early detection programs were conducted for cancers.

The top three cancers for men are prostate, lung and colon.

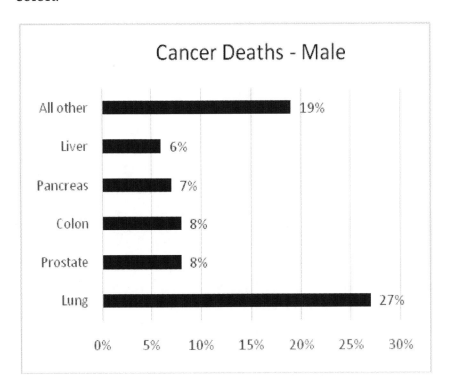

The top three cancers for women are breast, lung and colon.

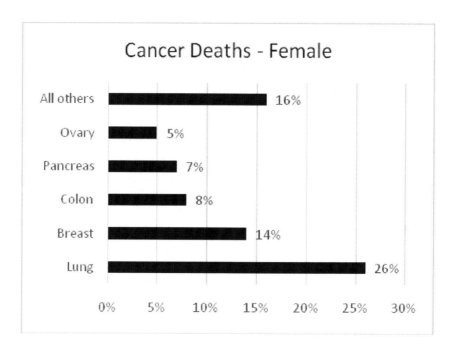

Lung cancer screenings are done via a low-dose computed tomography. This X-ray machine scans the body to take a detailed image of the lungs. Obviously not portable, employees must go to a clinic offering these services to be screened. Screening is only recommended for heavy smokers or those who have quit within the past 15 years and are over 55.

Colon cancer screening is recommended for employees over 40 using a fecal occult blood, FOB, card. The employee collects the sample at home and mails the card in for testing. The screening checks for blood in the stool and is considered effective since both polyps and colorectal cancers can bleed.

In recent years, several studies have linked low vitamin D levels with an increased risk for several types of cancer. A 2012 study found that vitamin D inhibits the growth of many kinds of cancerous cells, including breast cancer.

While testing vitamin D levels is not a cancer screening, knowing your level is obviously very important, and keeping your vitamin D levels optimized has obvious health benefits.

Problems from vitamin D deficiency include heart disease, birth defects, depression, hypertension, and stroke. Low levels have also been linked to dementia, fibromyalgia, impaired bone mineralization, skin, breast, prostate, and other cancers.

It is estimated that over 1 billion+ worldwide are deficient and we are finding that over 70% of the people we test are deficient, with 94% falling below the optimal level.

Interestingly enough, because so many Americans are testing deficient, the deficiency level was lowered in recent years from 32 to 30. The current recognized optimal range is50 to 70, with higher recommended levels for those diagnosed with heart disease or cancer.

Low vitamin D levels are also associated with poor asthma control. One Canadian study showed people with low vitamin D levels were 50% more likely to develop asthma. A Spain study found a 6% reduction of asthma risk in children for each 100 hours spent in the sun each year.

Prostate cancer is the second leading cause of cancer deaths in men, with one new case of prostate cancer being diagnosed in the U.S. every 2.4 minutes. The blood test to screen for prostate cancer in men is called Prostate Specific Antigen, or PSA.

While the PSA test is not perfect, and can be elevated for a variety of reasons other than cancer, both the American Cancer Society, and the American Urological Association agree to support individual informed decision making about whether or not to be screened.

Our pricing is so affordable for our clients, and even direct to consumers, that many opt to have the peace of mind of being screened.

Screening is done via a simple blood test that measures the level of PSA, prostate specific antigen, in the blood. PSA levels can be higher in men who have prostate cancer than those that do not.

Most prostate cancer is slow growing. Studies show that

the majority of men over 70 have elevated PSA counts. I have even heard a doctor say that if you live long enough as a man, you are going to develop prostate cancer, but you will probably die from another cause other than prostate cancer.

Nevertheless, it is a leading cause of death in men and needs to be addressed more seriously.

Another screening for early cancer detection is the CA 125 blood test, which is specific to ovarian cancer. We have had two women in the last couple of years that have had their ovarian cancer caught at stage one utilizing this test. Their doctors even say they would have never caught it at such an early stage. The cancer was still self-contained and they did not have to go through chemotherapy or radiation.

### 4.4.1 - Case study - Cancer screenings – a woman's story

For women, the CA-125 blood test can be used to measure the level of Cancer Antigen 125, a protein secreted into the blood by ovarian cells and often higher than normal in women with ovarian cancer. Though there can be false positives from this test, including those for pregnancy, endometriosis, uterine fibroids, liver disease, and benign ovarian cysts, Star Wellness® (the medical testing company owned by the author of this book) received this letter from a woman whose story makes the risk of a false positive worthwhile:

*"I had just completed my annual PAP exam, where my doctor did not catch a softball-sized tumor. My husband suggested we take advantage of the wellness testing and discounted pricing at his company. I remember being concerned that my bad cholesterol may be borderline high. But with my good cholesterol off the charts and my historically low blood pressure, my doctors told me I will outlive them all.*

*Then I received a call from Star Wellness. They suggested I call my gynecologist for follow-up as the number indicating ovarian cancer was greatly elevated. I saw my doctor and only 17 days after having blood drawn, I was in surgery. The CA-125 test caught my cancer so early (very early stage 1) that I did not have to endure chemotherapy or radiation.*

*My CA-125 will be tested quarterly for two years. So far it reads in the normal range. My doctor is well known for treating ovarian cancer and he tells me he shares my story whenever appropriate. He also now has a different perspective in regards to the value of CA-125 testing, knowing that false positives are common. He told me that his associates are also changing their perspectives on the value of the test in regards to early detection, in that they are experiencing more stories like mine.*

*I am grateful to my husband, to his company, and to Star Wellness for your service. Thank you!"* – Helen C.

## 4.5– Diabetes

Number four on our list is diabetes. Diabetes accounts for 10% of all healthcare dollars spent in the United States. According to the American Diabetes Association, in 2012 the total cost for diagnosed diabetes was $245 billion.

This represents a 41% increase from 2007, only a five year period. Obesity is the leading cause of Type II, or adult onset, diabetes. Search the internet for "The State of Obesity" and you can view maps of the U.S. showing obesity at the state level.

Over 29 million Americans are diabetic. One in four is not even aware that they have diabetes. More than 1 in 3 adults in the U.S., 86 million, have pre-diabetes! Of these, 9 out of 10 do not realize they are pre-diabetic.

Diabetes is also the leading cause of blindness.

Check out these stats about the increase in diabetes diagnoses in the U.S. since 1980:

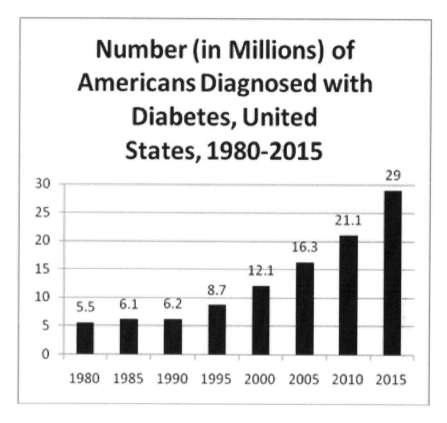

This is a very important category for employers to monitor since diabetic employees cost an estimated $8000 more per year in healthcare expenditures than non-diabetic employees.

That is a significant number, especially when you consider that for every 100 employees, 38 are overweight and 6 are already diabetic!

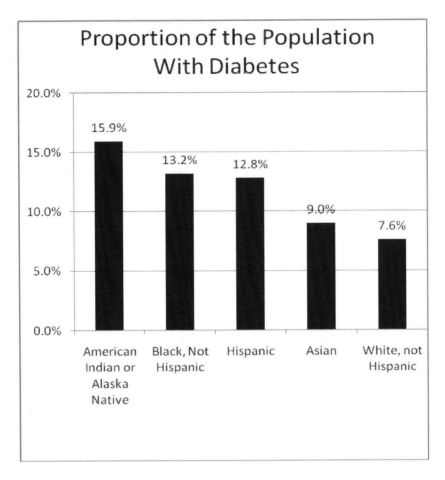

Before developing type 2 diabetes, you are pre-diabetic, meaning you have higher than normal blood glucose levels. The Diabetes Prevention Program (DPP) study conclusively showed that people with prediabetes can prevent the development of type 2 diabetes by making changes in their diet and increasing their level of physical activity. They may even be able to return their blood glucose levels to the normal range and STOP the progression! Studies also show that diet and exercise work better than medication for prediabetes.

Walking is a great way to start incorporating more movement into your day. For the first week, just walk 10 minutes a day, then work your way up to 30 minutes or more each day.

Studies show that controlling diet and moderate exercise is actually more effective than prescriptions, though often, people just go straight on prescription medications. I hate seeing diabetics who think, "Oh, well it is okay, I can go ahead and eat this piece of cheesecake. I'll just take more insulin." By not thinking through or understanding the impact this has on the body, they just inject more insulin to keep their glucose in the range their doctor suggests.

Fasting glucose is the screening that is generally offered for diabetes screening. Glucose is simply your blood sugar level at that particular moment in time. Having elevated blood sugar concentrations over time results in damage to the kidneys, eyes, nerves, and blood vessels.

The American Diabetes Association recommends that all abnormally high blood sugar tests (taken while fasting) be followed up with more detailed testing for a definitive diagnosis. When sugar becomes chemically bound to hemoglobin in the blood, a compound called Hemoglobin A1C (glycohemoglobin) is formed.

Historically, this test has been used to manage the long-term treatment of known diabetics and is used as an indicator of diabetic control. The A1C is also useful in identifying undiagnosed diabetics in the non-fasting environment commonly encountered at employee health fairs.

Hemoglobin A1C levels of 4.5% to 5.7% are considered normal. The A1C goal for people with diabetes is less than 7%. If patients can lower their HbA1c numbers by any amount, they will improve their chances of staying healthy.

## 4.5.1 Case Study - Diabetes is the #7 cause of death in the U.S.

Workplace wellness screening routinely finds undiagnosed or uncontrolled diabetics. Below is one example from our success story files:

*"As the Benefits Manager for my company I am responsible for organizing the wellness program. Each year, we have a company health fair with free screenings for all employees and spouses. In 2008, my screening results showed that I had an elevated glucose level. At the recommendation of my vendor, I followed up with my doctor, who did further tests and told me I was diabetic. I now have my glucose under control, have made changes to my diet and workout on a regular basis. I credit my wellness program to making a huge difference in my quality of life because I would have never even known I*

*was diabetic otherwise."* – Connie S.


## 4.6 - Thyroid Disease

Number five on our list is thyroid disease, which has been called the most undiagnosed disease in the U.S. It causes the body to use energy more slowly or quickly than it should and it affects more women than men.

Your thyroid gland is located in your neck on either side of your esophagus, below the Adam's apple in men.

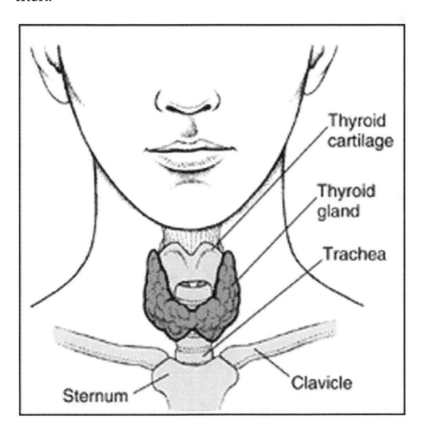

If you have thyroid disease, it can cause weight gain, fatigue, difficulty dealing with cold temperatures, cold hands and feet, hair loss and even cracks in your heels. The treatment involved attempts to reset your body's metabolism to a normal rate since the thyroid regulates the metabolism. While the majority of people who test out of range have hypothyroidism, where the thyroid is underactive, it is not uncommon to have hyperthyroidism, which involves an overactive thyroid.

There are a couple of tests that can be offered. Using ultrasound to scan the thyroid is quick, simple, and painless, performed while laying on a massage table. We have actually found cancer as a result of this screening, including in one of our own employees, while scanning as a demo for a client. We noticed an abnormality and sent films to our Radiologist for review, who recommended follow-up testing.

We have a couple of other stories surrounding thyroid findings as well. One was a client that was on the fence about whether or not to offer the screening to her employees. I offered to have her come by the office for a screening so she could see what it entailed for herself.

It was a similar situation, we noticed some nodules in her thyroid. We sent it to the Radiologist who recommended a follow-up study. So she went in and her doctor ordered another test, which came back inconclusive. He then ordered a biopsy. At this point she thought, "Oh, my gosh, this is costing the City so much money and it is a complete waste of time!" It came back inconclusive again so her doctor recommended surgery to be safe.

She had the surgery and the pathology result came back as thyroid cancer. Now she's one of our biggest screening advocates.

They decided to offer the screening for their group. She sent an email to the employees that the screenings were going to be available and then added, "Now for my personal story". She credits us for saving her life because she would have never known otherwise. Her doctor also told her he would never have caught her cancer in such an early stage during a routine examination.

There are several thyroid blood tests for thyroid, but the one we most typically offer as part of workplace wellness is the TSH, or a Thyroid Stimulating Hormone, because if your TSH is out of range, it can indicate whether there is hyper or hypothyroidism.

## 4.7 – Obesity

Obesity is a very important topic due to its prevalence, not only in the U.S., but throughout the world. There are many key factors that play a role, making it a somewhat complex issue to address. Being overweight is classified by a body mass index, or BMI, of 25 or higher. Obesity is defined as a BMI of 30 or higher.

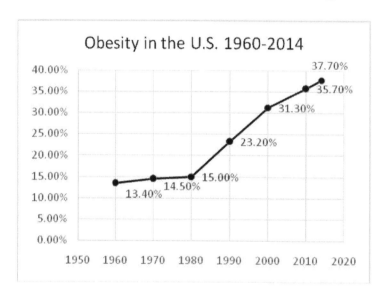

Over the past few decades, obesity in Americans has been increasing at an alarming rate. According to the National Institute of Health, more than two-thirds of adults are considered overweight, with over one-third of U.S. adults being obese. More than one in twenty adults are extremely obese (BMI over 40).

Unfortunately, obesity is also associated with an increased risk of heart disease, type II diabetes, cancers, high blood pressure, elevated cholesterol, stroke, liver and gallbladder disease, sleep disorders, respiratory problems, osteoarthritis and others. The CDC estimated that the national cost of obesity from 2008 was $147 billion. In 2015, no state had a prevalence of obesity less than 20%. The medical costs for obese employees is $1,429 higher per year than employees of a normal weight.

So what is body mass index (BMI)? It is a height-weight calculation – the formula is your weight times 703 divided by your height squared. The result is a mathematical ratio. If it is below 25, 24.9 down to 18.5, it is considered normal, if it is below 18.5, you are actually too thin. If it is above 25, you are overweight, and if it is above 30, you are considered obese. A BMI above 40 is considered extremely obese.

BMI is not accurate for certain athletes or bodybuilders because they will weigh more in proportion to their height due to increased muscle mass, not body fat. Because of this discrepancy, when we are screening for outcome-based programs, we use body fat percentage instead of BMI.

Overall, BMI is readily accepted as the standard measurement for obesity.

Most overweight participants already realize they are overweight, so people are not too surprised when we review their results with them. Unfortunately most Americans are somewhat overweight and need to lose a few pounds.

The way you screen for obesity is through height, weight, and waist circumference measurements. On our reporting, we color code results for easier comprehension. If results are in the normal range, it is colored green; high results are colored red, to flag as an area of concern.

Waist circumference is measured using a tape measure around the waist at the navel. While called waist circumference a more appropriate name is girth.

Recommended healthy results are below 35 inches for women and less than 40 inches for men. Over 40% of the participants we routinely screen have a high waist circumference, with the total percentage of women being slightly higher than men.

## 4.8– Stress

The last item on our list is stress. It seems that everyone is under stress nowadays. Technology has provided us with tools that are supposed to save us time, which it does to a degree. The real problem is that we do not end up with any time saved because instead of enjoying the time savings we just add more to our list, thereby creating a higher stress load.

If we were to use technology the way that it is marketed to us as a timesaver, then we would all have time to do anything we needed to get done during the day! Instead, we tend to fill up all of our time every day and live in a state of chronic stress, which causes a plethora of other problems.

According to the American Institute of Stress, the relationship between heart attacks and job stress are well acknowledged. One health concern for people with chronic stress is high blood pressure.

A March 2012 Business News Daily report showed that nearly half of all workers suffer from moderate to severe stress while they are at work, with 66% of them saying it affects their ability to focus on work tasks. That is an alarming statistics – two-thirds of the workforce says that they are under so much stress at work that they do not have the ability to properly focus on their job! In some industries or jobs, this can create a life-threatening situation if ignored.

The estimated cost of stress in the workplace to American businesses is $200-$300 billion a year. That represents a huge impact. Stress is also responsible for accidents, missed days, employee turnover, lateness, and errors.

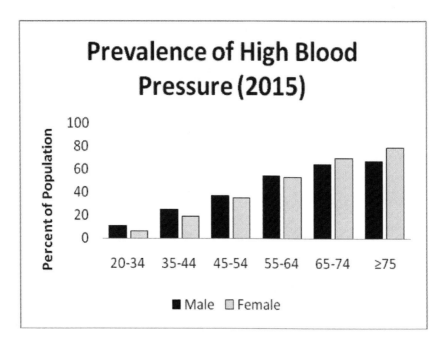

Incorporating stress related questions into your employee health risk assessment is effective in identifying stress among workers. Monitoring blood pressure is another tool to use and should be included in any onsite wellness screening.

A 2010 American Heart Association study estimates that almost 75 million Americans have high blood pressure, but only 78% of people are even aware it is an issue, and less than 64% of them are actually doing anything to control their blood pressure.

Blood pressure is a measurement of the force your blood exerts on blood vessel walls as it travels through your body. Your blood pressure reading is expressed with two numbers - for example, 110/70. The first number, known as systolic blood pressure, is a measurement of the force your blood exerts on blood vessel walls as your heart pumps. The second number, known as diastolic blood pressure, is a measurement of the force your blood exerts on blood vessel walls when your heart is at rest between beats.

Normal blood pressure for adults is below 120/80. If you are an adult and your blood pressure is 140/90 or higher, you have high blood pressure and should follow up with your personal physician. High blood pressure is one of the most common causes of stroke because it puts unnecessary stress on blood vessel walls, causing them to thicken and deteriorate, which can eventually lead to a stroke. It can also speed up several common forms of heart disease.

Doctors have long called high blood pressure "the silent killer" because you can have high blood pressure and never have any symptoms. If left untreated, high blood pressure can lead to life-threatening medical problems such as stroke, heart attack or kidney failure.

According to the American Heart Association, high blood pressure can occur in children or adults, but it is more common among people over age 35. It is particularly prevalent in African-Americans, middle-aged and elderly people, obese people, heavy drinkers and women who are taking birth control pills. It may run in families, but many people with a strong family history of high blood pressure never have it. People with diabetes mellitus, gout, or kidney disease are more likely to have high blood pressure.

Many health plans are now designed to cover blood pressure and diabetes maintenance medication at no out of pocket cost to employees. There are many generic medications available that cost as little as $4 or $5 a month. Employers recognize the benefit and potential cost savings of controlling high blood pressure and diabetes for such a low cost. Four dollars a month to keep an employee's blood pressure under control is far less than the potential claims costs of someone having a stroke!

The life expectancy for those with high blood pressure is reduced by 5.1 years for men and 4.9 years for women when compared to the life expectancy of those with normal blood pressure.

Aromatherapy is another area that has gained traction in recent years for reducing workplace stress. The response has been so overwhelmingly positive that many hospitals now incorporate aromatherapy in their waiting rooms and employee areas to reduce stress for both patients and employees. The cost for a diffuser and oils is minimal, with the added side benefit of a pleasant smell. Numerous studies are ongoing so this will be an interesting area to watch.

## 4.9- Workplace Vaccinations

While not included in our Sinister 7 list for early detection and prevention of disease, we would be remiss if we did not include workplace vaccinations in this section. Flu and pneumonia, which is frequently developed from having the flu, is the eighth leading cause of death in the United States, totaling approximately 50,000 people each year. A flu shot is the best protection from the flu and its related complications.

According to the Healthy People 2020 report, flu shots are "a very cost-effective clinical preventive service". Workplace vaccinations have gained popularity over the past decade, as preventive vaccinations are now covered100% by insurance.

Flu shots cause antibodies to form in the body for the viruses contained in the vaccine. It takes about two weeks to become effective and lasts several months. The viruses included in the flu shot change each year as manufacturers work to match the individual strains for the upcoming season. The CDC recommends that everyone over 6 months of age receive a flu shot each year.

To vaccinate your employees, find an in-network vendor for your health plan and an onsite clinic can be scheduled with no out-of-pocket cost. It is a true win-win. Employees appreciate the convenience and employers get better utilization and more widespread protection.

It is estimated that anyone who goes to work with the flu will typically infect four co-workers. Flu is highly contagious and grows exponentially very quickly. This is the reason we sometimes see schools closing down when they have an outbreak of flu or whooping cough. There have been entire school districts that had to completely shut down because so many employees and children were out sick. Yet another example that drives home the importance of preventive vaccinations.

Flu shots are very easy to get, typically at no cost to the employee or the employer when using a reputable in-network vendor who can file a claim.

During flu season, sanitize door knobs, light switches, & high traffic area regularly, provide hand sanitizer, and encourage employees to wash their hands often to reduce the spread of flu.

While there will always be employees who opt not to participate for a variety of reasons, we support the right of individuals to make an informed decision. Providing educational material that presents information in an informative and neutral way can help employees decide.

Other vaccines, such as Hepatitis and Tetanus, or TDAP, can also be provided via onsite clinics for employees who need them.

## 4.10 – Metabolic syndrome

Another important factor is Metabolic syndrome. It is the name given to a group of risk factors that increase your risk for heart disease and other health problems, such as diabetes and stroke. Metabolic syndrome has become increasingly common in the United States and worldwide. It is estimated that over 50 million Americans have metabolic syndrome.

The dominant underlying risk factors for this syndrome appear to be abdominal obesity and insulin resistance. Insulin resistance is a generalized metabolic disorder, in which the body cannot use insulin efficiently. Metabolic syndrome is also called the insulin resistance syndrome.

Any onsite screening provided to employees as part of your wellness program should include, at minimum, all five risk factors for metabolic syndrome.

The American Heart Association and the National Heart, Lung, and Blood Institute recommend that metabolic syndrome be identified as the presence of three or more of the following components:

| Large waistline | Waist measurement more than 35 inches in women;40 inches in men |
|---|---|
| Higher-than-normal triglycerides | 150 or higher |
| Low HDL ("good") cholesterol | Less than 50 in women; 40 in men |
| Higher-than-normal blood pressure | One or both of the following: |
| | 130 mm Hg or higher (top number) |
| | 85 mm Hg or higher (bottom number) |
| Higher-than-normal blood sugar | Fasting blood sugar 100 or higher |

The primary goal of clinical management of metabolic syndrome is to reduce the risk for cardiovascular disease and type 2 diabetes. Then, the first-line therapy is to reduce the major risk factors for cardiovascular disease: stop smoking and reduce LDL cholesterol, blood pressure, and glucose levels to recommended levels. Any increase in HDL, or "good" cholesterol levels, is considered beneficial. The most effective way to raise HDL levels is exercise. Most cholesterol medication, or statins, only lower LDL, or "bad", cholesterol levels.

For managing both long- and short-term risk, lifestyle therapies are the first-line interventions to reduce the metabolic risk factors.

These lifestyle interventions include:

- Weight loss to achieve a desirable weight (BMI less than 25 kg/m2)
- Increased physical activity, with a goal of at least 30 minutes of moderate-intensity activity on most days of the week
- Healthy eating habits that include reduced intake of saturated fat, trans fat and cholesterol

According to the Department of Health & Human Services, "Metabolic syndrome is becoming more common due to a rise in obesity rates among adults. In the future, metabolic syndrome may overtake smoking as the leading risk factor for heart disease.

It is possible to prevent or delay metabolic syndrome, mainly with lifestyle changes. A healthy lifestyle is a lifelong commitment. Successfully controlling metabolic syndrome requires long-term effort and teamwork with your health care providers." Employers can certainly, and should, play a role in this area as well.

# Chapter 5 - Building a case for wellness programs

## 5.1. More about the rationale

These days, companies are all about their people. In the past, management's focus was, and needed to be at various times, on equipment, access to resources, information, and technology.

Business has evolved, and now corporate focus, while still involved in these other arenas, is most often targeted on having the right people and seeing that they are performing at their optimum capabilities.

This entails looking after the well-being of employees and even encompasses initiating creative approaches to make sure those caring for aging parents have support. It includes helping employees with the inevitable transformations that occur in their lives and it involves helping employees to grow, come alive in meaningful ways, find happiness, and enjoy health.

The top challenge for corporations around the world is ensuring that employees are well and happy, because as we all know, healthy employees are not only happier overall, they are more productive employees as well.

An important part of any corporate wellness initiative is the experience and talents of outside vendors. They not only bring their expertise, but also provide peace of mind regarding confidentiality to employees. It can be difficult to find one vendor to meet all your wellness program needs.

Human resources personnel can look for specialized consultants who provide training — whether fitness or self-defense or meditation — as well as medical testing and screening, and counseling for those who have medical issues. Having different vendors who specialize in different areas avoids the "fox in charge of the henhouse" scenario as well.

## 5.2. Bigger is not necessarily better

How much money and time does a corporation need to invest in a wellness program to make it successful? Having a well thought-out program, with appropriate activities for your workforce and relevant rewards and incentives, may be a greater indicator of success than how much money you spend.

Having executive buy-in and support goes a long way. Making sure to involve an employee representative or representatives will also help morale. And continuing the program, with periodic uptakes of attention, is more important than a big initial splash.

After all, wellness should be viewed more as a marathon than a sprint. Eating one chocolate donut does not ruin health long-term any more than jogging at lunch for a week does not make up for years of overeating and smoking.

As in most things, communication is vital. Communicating through more than one channel will ensure that employees are kept informed, and hopefully motivated, to become and stay engaged. Videos, emails, voicemails, flyers, lunchtime talks, and contests are just some of the viable channels.

Online portals are also becoming popular, and even essential, for effective wellness program management. For a modest fee per employee you can have everything you need to efficiently run your program in one location.

An integrated portal can seamlessly consolidate health and wellness information for employees and increase participation. Everything is in real time, so confidential reporting is seamless and up to date.

The portal does all the tracking for participation and points for you. It enables you to delivered targeted messaging when necessary, all while remaining HIPAA compliant and confidential.

Employees can complete their Health Risk Assessment, review their biometric screening results, and download benefits information all within one portal. With third party integration you can even have claims information available.

Best of all, you own the data. If you switch insurance companies for any reason, you take your data with you uninterrupted. This makes it far easier to track year over year compliance and calculate ROI.

## 5.3. Building Employee Awareness, Interest, Participation

Building awareness, trust and participation is an interesting topic that is vital to the success of any wellness program. I would say that the most important thing is ensuring and communicating management support of participation in the program.

It is crucial not only that management support the program, but that they also actively promote the program and personally participate as well. In the most successful program I have seen, the CEO was completely on board. Each year as a team, employees that qualify at the top level are awarded with an incentive trip. The CEO, and any of his qualified staff, also participate as time allows.

This program remains one of the most cost effective programs. They have saved millions of dollars, during a time when everyone else is struggling to deal with their aging and unhealthy workforce. While competitors experience double digit premium increases, they have actually received premium reductions because their employees have become healthier, thereby reducing their overall claim costs. That is a huge competitive advantage!

Early on, when wellness programs first began, almost all of them were participation based. As long as you participated in the program, you received credit, it was completely voluntary. For many of your employees, the company wellness program may be the only health care they receive during a calendar year.

After a few years, we started to see incentives being added to the wellness program design as a way to increase participation above the average rate of 30- 35%. Incentives do increase participation when properly structured for your group and culture. There really is no one size fits all incentive program.

Now we are starting to see outcome-based incentives and mandatory participation, generally in the form of higher insurance premiums for non-participation. This structure can take participation rates from the 50% range to even 90% or more.

There are some legal guidelines surrounding each of the incentive types that need to be taken into consideration whenever you start your program, and those unfortunately change from time to time based upon different rulings, or state. You need to be aware of them to ensure your program remains legally compliant.

Fear is one reason employees put off getting medical testing, or initiating a new, healthier lifestyle. Lack of time is often proffered as another, but in truth, most people manage time quite well when they are motivated to act. So there are other reasons likely at play.

Delaying decisions is one reason for procrastination — unsure which medical provider to access, unsure what questions to ask and what choices to make, we put things off. If you cannot make up your mind, you avoid the uncomfortable feelings that evokes by focusing on other, "more pressing" matters. But nothing should be more pressing than our well-being.

Technology often only makes it worse. Instead of making an appointment for a flu shot, we answer emails. Instead of going for a walk, we send texts or go on Facebook to catch up with friends. It would be better if we met our friends to play tennis, or go skiing, or take an aerobics class. Instead, we sit on the couch with our laptops, or lay in bed with our Smartphones.

A corporate wellness program can help ameliorate this tendency in a percentage of our workforce. By having many services onsite, and making healthy food readily available in the corporate cafeteria, we take some of the decision-making stress away.

All employees have to decide is to get a flu shot—where and when is solved for them. All they have to decide is to take a walk. A track around corporate headquarters is right there and some of their coworkers are already using it. All they have to decide is to eat a salad instead of two candy bars or a donut for lunch, and the salad bar is just down a couple flights of steps. When employees get in the habit of making healthier choices they tend to reinforce that habit at home with their family as well.

If only all our issues were this easy.

A well-structured program will also have multiple pieces. Some of the pieces that I think need to be included are a good communication and promotion plan, as well as an educational component, a biometric screening piece, a smoking cessation program, a healthy eating and nutrition component, and a health risk assessment. Your program may need other components depending on your population.

Smoking cessation is probably the easiest to explain because everyone knows that smoking is bad for your health. Where smoking programs fail is when they only allow for one smoking cessation program per employee. This does not make financial sense when you actually drill down and look at the numbers. Most smokers want to quit, but it is an addiction and the first time through the program may not necessarily work. A well-designed program will cover a smoking cessation program for however many times it takes to be successful.

Nutrition is another factor that is often left out. I personally believe most people want to eat healthy, they just do not know how. The mixed messages from advertising certainly do not help either. There is the low-carb diet, the high fat diet, Atkins diet, the "starve yourself" diet, there is even a cabbage soup diet, plus thousands more. People are confused, they do not even know where to start.

Are eggs good for you or bad for you? Well, they used to be bad for you but now they say they are good for you. Does eating food high in cholesterol raise cholesterol levels or not? Did I hear that several studies show no correlation between the cholesterol in your food and the cholesterol in your bloodstream, it is produced by your liver? It is just too much confusion for people!

Even the U.S. food pyramid is under controversy because the base of the pyramid is carbs and grains.

Current data disputes eating this many servings of carbs in a healthy diet. Now we have choosemyplate.gov to use instead.

The general consensus is that your plates should be 50% vegetables with some fruits and a modest serving of lean protein about the size of your palm, along with a small amount of starch. Fruit as a snack 1-2 times a day. It sounds easy enough, and it might be if you are eating at home, preparing your own meal. It is not as easy to follow if you are eating out or only have fast food options. Many Americans eat out multiple times per week or even per day.

Having a well-defined nutrition component within a wellness program goes a long way in helping employees to better understand the correlation between what they eat and their health. Just having a handout on healthy options when dining out can be beneficial. Nutrition is key.

Being physically active and incorporating moderate exercise into your day is also important. Exercise is often touted as the weight loss key, so people tend to think the best way to lose weight is to exercise more. But focusing solely on exercise can actually sabotage weight loss. Studies consistently show that your personal eating habits are far more important than how much you exercise when trying to lose weight. Nutrition experts say successful weight loss is really

80% diet and 20% exercise. It is impossible to exercise your way out of a bad diet.

Walking is an excellent way to incorporate more movement into your schedule. It is easy and uncomplicated and can be done almost anywhere—on a track, in a stairwell, around a corporate campus, or in the neighborhood. It is easy on the joints, and works for employees of all ages and genders. Walking does not require special equipment except for comfortable shoes, and it relieves stress.

Walking can get us somewhere and it can also relax us. It can be done in short periods of time, and can easily be monitored by the number of steps taken each day— either with a pedometer, an app, or a fitness tracker.

The treadmill desk has arrived at some offices in recent years, and employers are encouraging employees to use them during the work day. The treadmill runs at a slow, walking pace speed and has an adjustable workspace for your computer or notes. Employees simply walk on the treadmill while on conference calls or checking email. It is a great way to stay awake during those boring after lunch meetings and get moving as well!

Walking is fun and can be enjoyed alone or with others. The time and place is flexible, and participation is not dependent on weather or level of fitness. Walking can be done slowly or at a fast pace, in large steps or small, taking breaks throughout the walk or all at once.

Women who walk at least four hours a week show mood improvement, higher creativity, feel better overall, and have reduction in chronic disease risk. Encourage your employees to walk.

Yoga is another great way to increase movement and reduce stress. Hiring a part-time yogi to teach at your office is an approach that has proven successful across a wide spectrum of industries. Hard-working employees may need this mental and physical exercise that creates a synergy between mind and body, assists with breathing techniques and flexibility, and fosters calmness and consciousness.

In the workplace where stress, deadlines, and other pressures take their toll, yoga can provide the relief that leads a portion of the employee population to better health and productivity. Not everyone will participate, but for those who do, yoga is a proven method of tapping into a person's inner resources.

Fitness balls are good for encouraging and training better posture while sitting. Originally used for rehabilitating individuals with spinal injuries, these balls are sometimes used in place of chairs and definitely as fitness tools. The advantages are many — muscle strength and tone, flexibility, endurance, balance, coordination, help with back, hip, and knee problems, and for improving posture and core stability.

A ball is a simple, inexpensive tool. The challenge of maintaining one's balance on a round and mobile surface creates fun and fosters laughter, while stimulating reflexes and using abdominal and back muscles that are not needed to sit on a hard chair or bench. They even come available with fashion covers.

What can the employer do? Well, these balls are relatively inexpensive, so they can be gifted or rewarded to employees interested in participating in company-supported fitness. A fitness training class can be developed using these balls. Employees can be allowed to use them in place of chairs if there is enough room in their offices.

It is vital that you help employees understand the relationship between generating a claim, by going to the doctor, and how that translates to an expense for the company, potentially increasing premiums. If they do not understand how medical care/benefits costs impact the company financially, then they are not going to understand the importance of participating in the program or why the company wants them to be involved.

Co-pays have removed the awareness in this area. Prior to co-pays and HMOs, most insurance was a simple

80/20 plan which meant that the individual was responsible for paying 20% of the overall bill and insurance covered the rest. Then, HMOs came on the market with their low co-pays and people flocked to them in droves.

My first HMO plan had a $3 co-pay. I could go to the doctor any time and it would only cost me $3. Suddenly, everyone went to the doctor for anything that was wrong with them! This system trained people to go the doctor for things that they would not necessarily have gone to the doctor with before. They did not realize how much the total bill was because they only had to pay their co-pay. Now co-pays are typically in the $30-$40 range, but it is still less than 20% of the overall bill.

There has been a shift in recent years that is changing this perception called cost shifting. Most companies now offer a high deductible plan, where employees have a deductible of $2500 or more. The deductible works to essentially shift a large portion of the entire cost to the employee. Most healthy employees will not generate more than $2500 in total health care costs during a calendar year anyway. When the deductible is raised to the $5000 limit, less than 10% of employees will meet it during a calendar year.

People are essentially self-insuring with these high deductible plans, making this a key area for identifying and building employee awareness, interest, and participation with a creatively designed incentive plan.

You cannot change what is not measured. Often times, the company provided screenings or health fair will be the only form of healthcare an employee may receive. We hear all the time, usually from men, "I haven't been to the doctor in over 10 years" or "I've never had my blood pressure checked" or "I've never had my cholesterol checked before."This is astounding, especially when you are checking a 40-year-old employee and they have never been to a doctor as an adult.

You do not want them to go that long between visits. Most medical groups advocate an annual health exam. Communicating and educating employees of the fact that they are responsible for their own health is also key. My personal belief is that to achieve wellness and longevity, you do not want to be on six prescription medications to maintain optimal levels for cholesterol, blood sugar, and blood pressure. Rather, take care of yourself, eat correctly and exercise so you do not need to be on <u>any</u> medications at all. After all, if you do not take care of your body where else will you live?

Unfortunately, with direct consumer advertising in the U.S., the pharmaceutical industry advertises on prime time TV and people think that they can just demand a pill from doctors for a quick fix. Doctors feel like they have no choice but to write a prescription for fear the patient will go down the street to the doctor next door, who will. Direct to consumer pharmaceutical advertising has created a vicious circle.

Creating a well-designed communication plan around the launch of the program is also essential to success. Many employees may not even know what a healthy blood pressure reading is or the difference between so-called "good" and "bad" cholesterol. A "know your numbers" campaign that discusses each component to be offered during biometric screenings prior to the scheduled date will educate employees, making them more aware of the program components, and will increase participation as a result.

We have seen this create a healthy competitive spirit as everyone wants to be the healthiest, and have the lowest blood pressure. There may be two or three employees getting screened at the same time discussing their blood pressure numbers and BMI. Their competitive spirit creates an interest in good outcomes, they want to make sure that they are at least as good as or better than their co-worker. A healthy competitive spirit among employees can help.

Along the same lines, we have seen many successful team weight loss programs. It is another program that is easy to implement, with minimal costs. You simply form teams of 4 to 6 interested employees who register and compete against each other. It is amazing how the team environment and competition amongst your co-workers helps not only with accountability and compliance, but also is more sustainable. The accountability component is key. Team mates are more compliant in following their meal plans and not cheating. We have seen many teams get together and walk at lunch. They will make sure that each of them get their steps in for the day!

Having a different topic focus each month or each quarter is another strategy that works. It is said to take 21 days to create a new habit. We often we see a "maintain do not gain" challenge during the holidays. This is a simple program where people will weigh in before Thanksgiving and then again after the New Year, with the goal of not gaining any weight during the holidays.

Other topics of interest would be heart health, diabetes, the importance of adequate sleep, various weight loss challenges, blood pressure, and cancer awareness. There are also national health awareness months, so creating programs around those can be easy and beneficial as well.

# NATIONAL HEALTH OBSERVANCES BY MONTH

JANUARY
- Cervical Health Awareness Month
- National Blood Donor Month

FEBRUARY
- American Heart Month
- National Cancer Prevention Month

MARCH
- Colorectal Cancer Awareness Month
- National Nutrition Month

APRIL
- Oral Cancer Month
- Stress Awareness Month

MAY
- Skin Cancer Detection & Prevention Month®
- National Stroke Awareness Month
- National Women's Health Week

JUNE
- National Safety Month
- Men's Health Month

JULY
- UV Safety Month
- National Park and Recreation Month

AUGUST
- National Breastfeeding Month
- National Immunization Awareness Month

SEPTEMBER
- National Cholesterol Education Awareness Month
- Ovarian & Prostate Cancer Awareness Month

OCTOBER
- Domestic Violence Awareness Month
- National Breast Cancer Awareness Month

NOVEMBER
- American Diabetes Month
- Lung Cancer Awareness Month

DECEMBER
- International AIDS Awareness Month
- National Drunk and Drugged Driving Prevention Month

Incentives do help with behavioral change, but only if the incentive fits the workforce. You may have a manufacturing environment with a bunch of guys where a small incentive such as a baseball cap with the company logo on it generates participation. However, that may not necessarily work at a school district for school teachers.

We have one client that gives a $100 a month premium reduction for participation, but they also have a second financial incentive for outcomes.

If an employee does not use tobacco and meets certain outcome levels, they can earn up to $150 a month in additional incentive, for a maximum of $3000 in total per year if they qualify in all of the categories. The best part is that the program self-funds and the company has the data to prove it.

Year over year claims analysis shows their workforce actually got healthier as they got older. It is the same employees, but they are losing weight and keeping it off, becoming healthier overall. They are able to get off medications because of their improved health, thereby reducing pharmaceutical utilization. You hardly ever see that, they have actually reversed the trend just by having a properly designed incentive program for their group.

Read that paragraph again. This incentive structure is so well designed that employees will quit smoking, lose weight, maintain a healthy weight, and take any medication for compliance if necessary. They become healthier overall. Healthier employees are more productive and better engaged employees with fewer sick days and increased overall happiness.

## 5.4 Integrating change

Psychologically, we appreciate things more when we work for them, much more than if they are given as a gift.

That said, incentives and rewards do work. Some examples of items given by employers as incentives include Fit bits, exercise balls, gift cards, gym memberships, or company T-shirts. Larger incentives include monthly premium reduction or outcome-based incentives.

But the effort of exercising or eating a peach instead of carrot cake needs to come from the employees. Only then will change take hold and be embraced by employees as real change, as a labor of love. Only then will they be truly satisfied by their progress. Only then will they revel in having more energy, in fitting into their old smaller jeans, and in managing their craving for cigarettes without lighting up.

Most people would like to reduce stress in their lives or lose a few pounds. Many just do not know where to start. Structuring a program in small, manageable steps with various incentives along the way can help ensure success for employees and their wellness initiatives.

It is important to engage employees logically, socially, and emotionally...on as many levels as possible. Fully engaged employees are more likely to stay with transforming their lives, their health, and their well-being. Even if the transformation is seemingly minor, it will have impact.

# Chapter 6 Conclusion

Workplace wellness programs significantly improve employee health and positively impact a corporation's bottom line. This has been documented by numerous studies, including those supported by the Centers for Disease Control and Prevention.

It is best to cover a wide range of risk-focused programs to be most effective. The idea is to impact behaviors and minimize or eliminate risks. It is not even necessary to use state-of-the-art techniques, though many are doing so, such as including technology and relevant apps to provide information and influence behavior.

It is vital to maintain a worksite wellness program long-term to ensure that employees continue to make and maintain positive changes rather than shifting back to old negative actions. Short-term changes are certainly doable, but it is important for an organization to encourage maintenance of change on a long-term basis.

By improving the health of employees, these programs save money for companies through reduced healthcare expenses, lower insurance premiums, lower costs for disability payments, and fewer lost days due to illness and related sick leave. Productivity also increases, thus producing a positive economic effect.

My intent in writing this book is to create a guide that covers the necessary components of a successful biometric screening program. This includes creative ideas for incentivizing employees with inspirational stories and motivational concepts, and entertaining information on health topics, which can be passed on to employees by their employers.

Easily implemented and increasingly embraced, corporate wellness is an evolving force of change that will benefit your employees. It is inevitably cost effective, capable of providing a tremendous return on investment.

The key is to make everything convenient, intriguing, and of high quality. Your employees will respond to a program that is well conceived, well executed, and properly funded. The well-being of your company and its most precious asset—its people—demands no less

# Chapter 7About Star Wellness®

## What is Star Wellness®?

We are a Texas-based firm working with employer groups throughout the U.S. to provide onsite medical screenings and obtain biometric data. We provide feedback via group aggregate reporting, which allow companies to identify problem areas within their employee population. We have both corporate owned and franchised branches of the business.

Once the prevalence of specific risk factors is determined, we help our clients develop wellness strategies and programming to mitigate those risks as early and as effectively as possible.

By outsourcing services to us, you help assure employees of their privacy and allow us to do what we do best while you run your company and do what you do best. We run the screenings, provide private reports to each of your employees, and handle all the details of scheduling, testing, and analysis, allowing you to remain focused on your business.

Our clients include HR and benefits managers. The HR department is frequently tasked with finding and deploying a wellness program. Often this is most successfully accomplished through outsourcing, as wellness is not the prime activity for the organization.

**The Star Wellness mission is three fold:**
1. **To save lives by alerting individuals to undetected health conditions requiring attention.**
2. **To save money for our corporate clients through early detection and prevention of disease among employees.**
3. **To empower individuals to take charge of their health by providing access to their individual results.**

## Flexibility

Ours is not a one-fits-all program. Instead, we work with clients to help their employees, whatever their industry or size, creating a customized program that meets the needs for their group.

Businesses and organization now recognize that preventive care is the best way to control healthcare costs and improve productivity by reducing employee sick days.

# «. Praise for Star Wellness USA .»

"If you know your blood pressure, your cholesterol count, your glucose level, and other statistics, you are in a better position to modify what you eat and how you exercise to avoid or minimize the destruction that major diseases may cause. When your employer helps you obtain all the relevant numbers at your worksite in just a ten minute screening, that employer should be applauded." – David S., Director of Wellness

"We count on Star Wellness to always offer new and innovative ideas. They provide lab collection services and vascular screening for our 400 employees in Texas, Wyoming, Montana, and North Dakota. They also conduct yearly onsite flu clinics at our corporate office and support us with other immunization services as needed. They have certainly made our wellness program stronger and more attractive to participants." – Connie K, PHR, HR Benefits Manager

"Star Wellness is always set up and ready to go before our health fairs open. Their employees are well-trained, competent, and hard-working. My employees receive lab and screening results in the mail the same week in which they are drawn, and aggregate reports are provided to me in a timely manner. During one health fair, Star Wellness handled more than 600 lab draws and nearly 200 other health screens in a single day! Amazing company to work with..." – Kim T, RN, Employee Health & Wellness Supervisor

"Once the effective wellness motivations have been found and implemented, the results in your workforce can be amazing. Our wellness program is seven years old now. We have several different types of incentives for employees to earn both financially and with paid days off. We have seen the overall health of our employees improve. Since the first year, we have had a 500% increase in participation and the measured risk factors have been cut in half over the same time. Biometric testing, wellness seminars and physical activities all in combination have had tremendous success but we still have a ways to go." – Rick D., SHRM-SCP, PHR, IPMA-C, HR Supervisor – Benefits and Employee Wellness

"We LOVED having your team out for flu shots today! The company we had coming out for the past few years did not offer to file the insurance and employees had to pay out of pocket. Your team really helped make my (new HR rep) first flu clinic a success. We also had a number of participants talking about how their shots didn't sting as much as the previous years, which I believe was mostly based on the experience of the young man who administered the shots today. I loved the lady who helped complete the paperwork, she explained everything very clearly and was able to go over the "wow" factor that there is no cost to us. I literally could not be happier with how everything turned out. I will be writing a review online for your company, but wanted to reach out and personally thank you!"-- Lydia F, Manager of Human Resources

"As a business owner my biggest expense is medical insurance for my employees. Everyone should be focusing on the prevention side of health care and wellness throughout the business. Johnette gave me the education I needed on corporate wellness." – Terrence Shaw, MBA

# About the Author

**Johnette van Eeden** is an author, speaker, thought leader, and CEO of Star Wellness®, a Texas-based onsite medical screening and laboratory services company that helps employer groups implement wellness programs that control healthcare costs and promote employee well-being.

A former computer programmer, Johnette founded her company in 2003 after realizing that time and money was being spent on fitness and wellness programs without monitoring the effectiveness of these programs. She began offering cholesterol testing and other medical screenings to businesses, and was immediately in demand.

Through acquisition and expansion, her company now provides a full range of confidential, convenient, and affordable medical testing onsite for many school districts, municipalities, and corporations across multiple industries.

Ms. van Eeden studied executive management and entrepreneurship at Northwestern University's Kellogg School of Management, McComb School of Business at University of Texas Austin, and Tuck School of Business at Dartmouth College. She completed post graduate studies in Entrepreneurship from Biz Owners Ed, and is a graduate of Goldman Sachs' 10,000 Small Business training program.

She works hard in her business and devotes time to her husband and family, and has worked with children on a volunteer basis through Junior Achievement and Big Brothers/Big Sisters. She also donates free wellness services to low-income residents in her community and works with her local school district to provide internships for phlebotomy students.

Ms. van Eeden was recognized as an Enterprising Women of the Year finalist and her firm has been named as one of the top 15 fastest growing women-owned businesses in Texas. An inspiring motivational speaker, *Navigating Wellness* is her first book.

Johnette van Eeden, CEO of Star Wellness®, wrote this book to share what she has learned after more than a decade of providing onsite medical screening and laboratory services to thousands of individual employees across the U.S.

A recognized leader in the field, Johnette provides advice, insight, and perspectives on the trend toward the all-inclusive well-being of employees. In the process, her informative thoughts encompass health, fitness, nutrition, motivational change, behavior modification, and corporate management tactics and techniques.